Azad Ashim Sharma

Ashwani Sharma

Kashif Sharma-Patel

SUBURBAN FINESSE

Sad Press

Bristol 2021

978-1-912802-42-5

Pandemonium is suburbia, pure and simple. The rioters are speaking in perfect English.

Sean Bonney

Is stupid to why we're here, meeting after all these years in a country full of white people all at once, irregardless of the suburbs. Do you come from a suburb? I come from a ditch.

Bhanu Kapil

Introductory Notes

A movement in our collective thinking – our de / post / anti / non / colonial study as an on-going experimentation in/as ontological breakdown. Poetics as thought – as *un*thought. The diasporic thinker as poet at the limits, the postcolonial limits of language, reason, writing. If for Aime Cesaire 'poetry is knowledge,' ours is an episteme at the edge of intelligibility, in excess of the modern subject of history – we are the madness of the postcolonial inhabiting, transversing, haunting the imperial nation in rapid descent.

At the edge of diasporic (sub)urban being – an imperceptible in/visibility, an opacity to the violent racial fetish of brownness — haunting the neuro-fascism of the police state, the state of the situation — a secret, on the edge, losing one's mind — disappearing in the shining en-lighten-ment, undoing cartographies of white terror and death.

Sub/urban poetics re-tracing the topological movement of the subaltern, the slave, the coolie, the paki, the queer abject, as incalculable figurations, ethical ruptures, in the circuitry of racial capital in the aftermaths of urban modernity. Nahum

Chandler posits the 'Negro is a problem for thought' – thought is the problem(atic) for race, poetics, space.

The problematic is a limit, at a limit, and an opening, a spacing, a gap, a fissure, almost nothingness in which poetic language delimits. Non-being, appositional to the urban disaster, a collective nothingness that irrupts in the temporal logics of *para*-coloniality, to after the end, finitude and the infinite, transversing the histories, collective memories of loss, death, trauma, life, joy, sociality, hiding in the light. An elegiac lament as nothingness, invisibility, the *imperceptible* demand and refusal for opacity in the lightness of being — postcolonial madness as a twisting spiral, a vortex of dense poetics after the end, at the edges of urban control and violence.

Here are some entangled traces of improvised thought and/as/or poetics mourning and futurity – a broken lyricism for a sub/urban fugitivity.

Our hauntological study as the silences and sounds between the schizophrenia of being and words, between the inner and outer city.

Let the sub/urban riotous/righteous run amok. This is Outer London in the Black House – tracing a darker shade of communism ...

subtended quotidien

> Head freeing – out in front
> body numbed in painkillers
> and exhaustion
> a cocktail of distrust
> time vibrates in the nook of
> the bus's embrace
> a public unto itself

double graphic pole (after the kid)

        that start and end internecine
        text as life takes hold
        silence and interpenetration
        at the end of the book
        beginning the writing
        beginning the book
        begins the writing
        like a double graphic pole
        between desire and narrative
        and social actuality
        where becomings keep rolling –
        in that internecine space
        of writing and place

gully to gully

shard sold out and
elemental elocutions //
cosmopolitical characterisation
at the cross of Edgware Road
        and
Church Street as market wares
pass hand and cloth drapes
in bouts of cultural assertion
across the allure of the navel

Railway replacement service

For Gyan – neuro-diverse artist, and brother of Azad. One of our own. In response to Gyan's paintings. Living in Morden – suburban/south London.

grass verges lining minds, small
memories locked indifference
spinning in my head, curtains
twitching suburban drift,
national history. last days
of the raj, papadom please.

Kingfisher piss water drunk
across imperial lands, you're one us
brown as white, flashing colours,
I feel through the haze of
abstract expressionism, suburban
futurism,
red marx
at night. the terror

white suffocation, white light,
commuting without bowler
hats, speculating capital, flights of
fancy, another runway, no thanks
full English against the swarm
'I want my country back', kebab
and chips, Paki Taliban, veiled threat. leave the
chicken vindaloo. No. 93 whizzing framed
in my head, fragments

scattered, boxed out, painting the town
red, strokes against the grain. lines of
flight. window on the
world, through the looking glass,
caged out, freedoms, shades of blue, Jaipur
red city, shenai drones piercing
ear drums, Rajasthan express. I love India,
the vibrant colours,
the poverty, souls starving to death.

Mr Singh, a fine fellow, bus driver
father served in the army. coolie paki.
Norman Tebbit failed the cricket test.
would you like some mango chutney
with your puke? going round and round on the
south circular. Korean or
are they Chinese? Buddha of
suburbia Enoch's nightmare.

Sufi magic
in the hands, chromatic diffusion as resistance,
Adorno said so. whirling dervishes
jet airways, in/organic
intellectual in the white cube, breaking it
down for the suburban folk. translucent riotous
waves of deep blue rage, blurred excess of life
beyond the frame.

insomnia, words lost in utopia, uncle Salim's car
escape routes from cul-de-sacs. wrong side of the tracks,
fugitive
aesthetics, still life.

         postcolonial pop art,
 Mitcham's Basquiat, multiple photo-selves,
 brown Rothko, Warhol in the (sub)urban jungle,
 nail bars and chicken shops, Bollywood dances
 in the church hall. anyone for tennis?
 Don't mention the B word.

Dys-Structure Abyssal Mordune (Modern Finesse)

The breeze over
Canon Hill common
washes away
the rancour of midnight
frivolities into the dew
and this cobalt grey morning sun.

Back under *MORDUNE* -
the anglo saxon village
full of brooks from the Thames -
now crowded by electronic bazaars
and rivulets of song from the minarets
of our Ahmadi Masjid.

I sing the mordune electric,
bashful and low-lying,
a town intoxicatingly mundane,
and is there philology to answer
for this proximity or is there history
to account for resistance?
Division now tries to sow
in tarmac post-referendum fires
those which burn the mosque
but missed the prayer hall.

What palimpsest is this imaginary
where charred paint is the evocation
of subsistence as neoliberal identity:
is to be built from these lullabies
just caste iron wrought in sectarianism
or is belief something that brings hope
manifests in money from abroad saving face?
To make from carceral historicism
a cartography of the spatial hermeneutic
what intentionality could rebalance foundations?

I long for the new
marble development
the scaffold excites
w/ promises of pristine sober bodies.

Great hall of brown smiles:
Morden's limitless Aleph.

Ye old Irish bar stands opposite
the century next to a betting shop
a Pakistani-Bangladeshi collaboration
also known as a cabbies'.

Home for a fiver.
Home counties they tell me
discouragingly as I write.
What even counts as a home
if I was displaced in the eggs' aisle?

Inside one and the other the fusion
of freshly poured Guinness mixes
with the saag and clarified butter,
aromas over and under our lot
so now the morning commute
one appreciates this as the zone where we cusp on
to the garden & the concrete: Sunological –

Morden is to drink bitter with H. Hatterr
to philosophise or trade photos of rare stamps
& stop the English beating each other –
The football might be on but it's not that deep
like the river here is traversable,
thin on the ground,
yet reflective as your eyes were
when you turned to me
and said 'yeah I can get used to this' – Still.

I sing the morden finesse
at the edge of the northern line
southbound out of the window
in uncle Salim's whip inside the outside
Community of communities make
the sheath more ornate than swords
No room for bloodied metal
because without Mordune I do not exist.

My family were the first brown
family in this village within a village
Where morden lowers into Surrey,
where to be from a place
is to say so with apology.
As the City of London shuttles west and east
as north London grows closer to Leeds,
the South anchors this broken rudder
less place built by those the City kept
as second class subjects:
Was it not our black, brown, beige sweat
that oiled the rail tracks?

And if the ship is rudderless now
is it not-not a problem for us at all?
All these toddler diasporas talk
about roots and culture.
We set down a big fuck off anchor into the river.
        Motion continued
In our bodies and with our art
free of the direction of a failed city.

What makes a place as a space
this is the place of safety is it not?
Re-thought the performance
of the spatial dialectic
Brings out the chocolate and stains my teeth
with my neighbours' love
We share third party wall agreements
and more – we agree to disagree –
I receive your cards on Christmas, Eid, Diwali,
and my Nan's birthday.

Morden park at the rear of St. Lawrence's church
would give Wordsworth a hard on
stronger than the foundations
of over priced Cabins in the lake district.
Morden. Mordune. Mundane. Magnificent.

Morden is a big juggernaut dancing
In the Turkish café
Folkloric dehiscence

Please don't try and restore the liberal order
You can't contain the salad
Mo salah masala mo salah masala.

I sing the morden finesse with my cup of splosh
poached egg on marmite toast
I let your embrace gooseflesh my neck.
You welcomed the exiled & gave us a playground.

When some mug complained
to the TFL about the tube station book-swap,
we rioted quietly and went on strike
without complaints from Management.
For once they seemed to be on our side.
Now re-opened the book-swap thrives
brings magic to us, traces and skin
Feelings touching upon our community,
connecting without pretence.

As diffraction and as difference,
the morden finesse utters continuity
For Punjabi Glaswegian bus drivers of the 50s,
the charos in Finchley,
the forgotten histories of South Asian women who fought apartheid.

A department store worker in 1940's Jo'burg
    called my grand-aunt
a kaffir. She punched him in the face and got
    arrested. She was 14.
My uncle Dawood is rumoured to have pissed on
    an Afrikaner copper
As a child who grew up amongst demonstrations
    and resistance.
What kind of childhood do we have in exile?
What does it mean to have a feeling in the air
that you can consume as you breathe?

When the IdPol Cambridge graduates
      talk about decolonisation
      send them to Morden
      let them meet the people.
            Send them now.

When you talk more about race than anti-racism
I have this feeling that you're pulling the ladder up
& all you want is to be acknowledged / included.

When you forget metonymy
I get worried and reduced
Like a pan sauce over a bavette
or maybe chutneyfied in the liberal mango.

You can do all the self exoticising you want
Selling out your community
for fast cash and 'recognition'
But in the end you're wanking yourself off
And I'm sheltered in the corner shop
talking to some random uncles
About Samsung being better than Apple
But also how it doesn't matter
because we're all being listened to.
You said I didn't listen
Said I did too much telling for lack of showing.
Well fuck you and your new Instagram account.

Morden is not a sub disciplinary ghetto
if by ghetto you mean stuck
what was once isolated is made possible
and given form. Then allow
1926's station to decolonise Clapham
by virtue of real luck. Fuck yuppies
And bachelors in suits watching rugby
singing something about swinging low.

In Morden we can stand tall
before Anubis and travel light to the hills.

Morden as method is method
to rethink to ab-use Reason & all that.

Mordune is method as method
recalibrates poetry for social analysis.

Jaipur is the place overlaid
onto the Royal Surrey pub,
pink bricks
Inside and out,
Sun Ra plays backgammon with our Hanuman-Ji.

As fingers drum on the counter
maybe the monkey God turns
To you and says, Žižek is wrong you know,
about refugees, about us.
The simultaneous brought into the fore
ground of chequered blind spots.

Enter Morden the schizophrene patiently.
Good yout walks in the park.
Young veteran walks amongst bluebells
on the tricontinental road.

Describe the scene, the picture, the enframing?
I see trees on trees on trees
But I have been alienated
from these paths and don't know
Their names. I don't know when
the leaves change colour.
I cannot predict what the weather
will be like tomorrow.

All I know is that in Morden
it takes some finesse
and it has it
because the coffee shops round here
don't play loud music
& we can have this conversation.

Walk back to Morden Park and jump
over the brook. Is the river then
A border to the world?
This river comes from the Thames, right?
So the South *is* dys-connected.
The north has all the buses and trains.
All of this to say hence ghettoization?
How many London Mayors promise
line expansions to help us commute to work?
Fuck work and fuck the GLA.

In the South we don't worry about work.
We don't worry at all. We just do poetry.

We are poetry.

Fanon said: a single line is enough.
Caecilius est in Morden.

We don't do reasonable discussions round here.
We jumped the river. We jumped the barrier.

Morden asks us to strike a pose
I strike a match and inhale
Microplastics in solidarity
with intermixed subjectivity like fish.
A Fish is a fish brother.

If structuralism came here
as humanism it tried to jump
Over the brook and missed the other side.
Stand on the other side.
South London is after the future.

Gaze into the brooks' reflection:
radical technology of criticality.
Give Morden contrapuntal analysis
where hybrid identities are cyborgian ontologies.

What mordune ain't is what mordune is
And it sure as hell ain't raucous free jazz
We just have a low hum of submerged social noise
Little eddies of traffic partition oak from willow
In the damp conscious of posthuman geography
As post-London pours freedom from ailment.

Morden as *topos* welded to my spine as gratitude
Morden as the first verb I spoke just be-cause.
The peoples' republic of Mordune: let it breathe.

Tympan, or, listening to paintings

Tympan: Fr. ear drum, membrane, relationship between frame and text,
the limit and the other
Jacques Derrida

    noise of the city
        paintings scream
          traffic roars
            buses humming
              sonic cartographies
                noise pollution
                  sounds blurring
                  poetic notes
                    tower of babel
                      imperceptible capitalism
                    blue sirens
                      algorithmic music
                      sonic booms
                  turbulence
                  ambient
atmospheres

                    diasporic cacophony
                    ears vibrate,
                    oscillate, fluctuate
                    plugged in,
                    plugged out
                        head-phones,
                    phone-heads
                beats
                    migrant beats
                    two tone
                    urban jungle, grime

music

                                              me-pod. I-not we
                                              head music
                                              bass rumblings
                                              low frequency
                                              modulations
                                              heart thumping
                                              pneumatic drill

                                           bashment, Babylon
                                             wall of sound
                                            flesh vibrations
                                            eyes listening
                                          ears seeing
                                          ears blocked
                                          ears bleeding
                                       acoustic pressure
                                         digital drums
                                       metallic grinding
                                         shouting out
                                       suburban quiet
                                        radio silence
                                     invisible chatter
                                       white noise
                                       red shift
                                   blue note
                             secret whisperings
                         sound systems
                          bass lines
                          rub-a-dub
                         headspace pulsating
                         percussive bodies
                         after the noise
                         beyond the frame

                        invisible sounds
                         sufi utterance
                         sacred songs
                         soul music
                        social music
                       girl talk
                    queer rhythms
                    monkey chatter
                    hearing voices
                    keeping quiet
                         inner speech
                            muffled sounds
                                 make some noise
                                   loud speaker
                                      loud colours
                                         horns blaring
                                           riotous
chanting
                                           muezzin pray
calling
                                              voices
haunted
                                            deafness
deafening
                                      echo chamber
                              listen to the silence
                          quantum vibrations
                       nothing, void, infinity
                     dark\matter, big bang

can we hear the subaltern paint?

Prefossilised Life

      In that calcifying movement
      where Thorpe's Park revelries inculcate
      into the Pink City's splendour where
      street vendors jostle for clout and
      buses trundle along elephant pathways
      as if the colonial's retreat into John Lewis
      predates the New, where Delhi
      collapses under Maruti smog
      – prefossilised life –
      jet streams and Jet Air

                      We are lost revelling in buses heading
                      outta Modern - Outer Pradesh's
                      pensive cousin

In the blur

In the blur of a turban's
presence the elephants stand still
intransigent to their flight//
multiplying nodes of cybernetic
undergrowth trace past –
in terrific bursts of animal spirit
where Uncle Salim's car interior
disperses into frenetic filialities
at the breaking point of the cerebral
we move disjointed// in tandem//
in slipstreams of improbability
covered nape to toe in Jaipuri razais
awash in colour //

we devised new maps

disrepute

At the centre of elephant

urban myths of much repute

        – aphex twin / colonial centre / chaplin's

      mausoleum / shakespearean haunts –
                            all SE's
                    finest

new flats asunder as pop-ups inchoate
delancy and sadiq - robber barons dispossessing
blue fading fronts, rude swaminarayan passing out tea
biryani, chicken specials, keralan beef curry,
faux-gold jewelry / black cowboy waffles / -ing

                                    england
                                sanitising

Good Friday

        freewheelin handsworth
        'land that forgot time'
        racist roundabout pubs
        where african village now stands
        the roads gone global
        kurds czechs and all supping on golden pastry
        bearded men and their gilded windows
                suburban bliss
        southern leafy climbs sitting with ice cream
        perusing the last remembrances
                new memories
        balti legends trail from mountain life
        into industrial territory
        sangam original dining
        impromptu seasonability
        the original queers
        that old trans shop with big shoes
        where global food market marks change
        and moving on make possible.

the ends festival, croydon

Get Out (2018) malfunctioned multiculture
in hemorrhaged gujurati households
roads closed, interloping groups
scamper in june splendour
'get away from that lot,' we hoped
littering maccy-dees like capsules of good fortune

tooting streaks

blinding impreciseness
quick transactions
lounging work

bus stop
heavy lifting
too hot, piping up
gold chain for a lively one
the elders chime on
too hot, ghana today,
on my feet for 9 hours,
dangerous now,
thieving youths,
my arches gone, no can do,
oh the kidnapping
quickly away, depart, dispense
streaking off amicable

Southern Finesse

I

sexual cut

bookshop

eatery

                the realisation of myth/desire/placidity
                    inner city bustle /
                          indian movement /
                  african freedoms /
                                legibility

    elephant thameslink

II

> croydon postdubstep imaginings intermixture
> striated cafes and born-again promises
> tamil eelam boardings, little beiruts, kurdish dreams
> six foot dosas and gold coast promises

III

       brixton 90s style and slick / buses business /
dark climaxes and ruined markets / u no im not bein
rude bt u no y i dont say it u no / *white ppl* u whisper /
arab-african men slurping soup in reverse engineered
elocution subtle and sufficient / opposite romanian
panini sellers

IV

    meetups in pubs gleaming
    overwritten floors and
    overbearing lighting
    aging melodies still adamant
    as chairs upheld in righteous
    inertia, gossip rings true
    in throats laced with current abandon

                    we left content, in control
                    queuing for grub and hospitality,
                    streets ridden with flesh and shadow
                    incredulous aunt's practicing kantian
                    judgement
                    in morning gupshup

Interlude: We blare it indestructible (Morden Finesse)

So we to morden? | soweto-morden !
the body is a body we blare it indestructible
lay all of it down in the budge
play chipinga from bricky's sound system
one thing about this hybridity
when it hits you, you feel all right –

call me a british bulldog like nehru
with that port of natal nonchalance
then our music emanates essence
and my afrindian cheeks move –

I was doing road in morden
when my frontal lobes changed shape
from crapulence to stentorian shahadah
abruptly recalling to me those khaki suits
strolling in the sky over haifa
when everything is under lockdown
but this fire this poetry this body bun
it lets the clip ring from our straps
as we stormed westminster without papers –

coda:

I ask Bhanu-ji how to wash my heart
she taught me to get out of asking
questions to move through the world
and when 'you're out of it dear person'
you will find yourself / myself with my heart
in my hands I found the salve
under all the decay I saw silver blood
to breathe in the day with this body indestructible.

is there football on i can leave you with?
newsnight's on
oh great, that's basically football for the world
yeah theatre of dreams, didn't
adorno say something like that?
nah i'm pretty sure that's old trafford

      narco   narky   lark
      nattering in   thames
      polis   down

garba in-script

religious doldrum
overexpectant returns
re-evaluative returns
durational faculty
rejubilant surrogacy
sanctity

        the re   -   turbulent

        field   in   monotonous

        entrapments   sat tightly

        in   confidence satiated

        spilling circles of parse   -   ness

bedouin errings
in the slur of spring whip wind
half step contained walks
in fragranced contrast
the half brothers and parish
families cut across cloth

       halfspoken toilet ushers
       in bellicose floors
       misapprehending alignments

                          creaking breezy words flying
for the postexpectant gratuitous slumberers where
                    worldly   irritants   pale   in
pusillanimous chuntering ushering in futures implicit

plumstead motion sickness semi detached marquees patio
premature mike leigh suburban dreams   – veg biriyani / chips
at morley's / momos at kailash / vine tomatoes on the go /
himalayan abodes – blessings in oil down axioms / separative
foods / in shredded chicken and salt beef and sweet breadfruit
/
local honey to whom / outercity journeys with manosankar

urban recall (after anti-caa protest)

to exhibit
        exhibit the scene
        say it twice / twice
we say it twice
in
        kabirnagar
we say it twice
exhibit the line
we say it twice
we learn and exude
        pervade
we learn and say it twice
        shahdara
we say it twice
we study and say it twice

i said it twice and the
        liver expelled bile like
        maruti exhausts re-engineer
        and retro-fit ambassadorial outings
they said reference properly, explain
we said it twice
noone literal, but to the oriented
garb, the garish jumble

clashing

I

soundclashes in forest vestiges
gotten ashes fever
short leg gully encroaching
    leg slip behaviour
forgotten clashes in dancehall fever
wapping passes – parties , parses
vegan encroachments at
    marie's cafe //
    tofu sidling drunken noodles
    beckoning chrysanthemum teas
white girls and foregone roles
(als)

vomit-flecked lawlor copy, hard back form, they call them

that came out of my nose

    great british porridge
        found glory in packets
        of quinoa and jarred

        butter beans
        village - styled

autodidactic evenings
        emails drafted
        supple interests
        make it happen

II

reeling in – were
firming up gold like
crown dirging down
flailing in like a
burning dream durga dream
deathly dream dura durgha
dusty ass tentacular
octacular adumbrating

III

carni vibes
post summer
stokesy thing
float systems
scorcher

guava disaronno
water chana dall
wasabi peas banane

        ecological mass
        atmospheric masses
        aesthetic alliole corpuscles
        plastic cups passing hands
        swilling over head crunch
        gurl thing gal thing
        rose-d cheeks concealer rouge
        cap and sunnies

lost signals lost folks
bloody stories basic channel
noon at gladdy wax

palpable errings

                    imaginatory
            data thief over yonder
                masterful womack
                  fuelling tellings
                      peripatetic tales
                over the city
                      find breathe
            grabbing throat
            callbacks
                behind the bar
'cant believe to be seen / it will never be the same'
                        george panayiotou is history

De-Presse: MeMe Noir (Modern Finesse)

Zero vibes just smart phones and stupid people
I ain't felt alright in a while now
arguing with all the liberals and tories
it's exhausting and the betting shop
full of unofficially employed rudeboys
is just the place for me
putting all my pain into the roulette
and turning it into chance: how surreal.

Out of the tube station it is a ruckus
orderly queues for buses to Brixton and Croydon
all I see are people of colour and of class
standing side by side waiting to be inspired
or given an exit strategy from this nightmare.

Wake up and work,
work from home,
live at work.
Shuttled into the day
like sardines pre
served by l'etranger sweat
a suburban delicacy:
we are all in a pickle init.

Don't get me wrong
French sounds lovely
a bit of pain and vin and boursin
but when you chat
about enfant terrible in your riddims
you just sound out of touch, bourgeois.

Morden needs its own bard
and I'm ready to call it on for this town
a ticket and a Guinness and wait
was that Linton Kwesi Johnson
strolling on the platform at Balham?
My Mrs checks on google
and dumbstruck and fucked up
Looking at my shoes contemplating
the strategy left out before me
by those dapper dons
celebrating lack of employment
in memory of Darcus Howe
because we don't wanna make money
by the means decided for us by the state.

If political blackness makes a comeback
just smash a liberal with a champagne bottle
smash a tory with a prosecco bottle
just rush a fascist and we can bout it talk later.

I'm done with using convoluted expressions
when I need to talk to the people of Morden.
I'm done with the ism and schism
London is the problem; The City is Babylon.

Finesse as depression but I cyan finesse de press.
Solemn as a lobster I walk past the asda
watching the salmon sky slap me: tawba tawba.
We stan with the upriser against the usurper
legalize we don't represent we don't diverse we.

As object I move through grotesque normality
devastated by the simple point of existence
discontent and restless and irritable
trying to have fun with a stepping razor
that I've turned against myself
to flay my own flesh so I can fit into society.

Capital is the Op I don't pray for
and I found philosophy on the high road
by Mitcham's cedars I sang
a redemption song for the liberation
I want to be free from deletion
The end of the line is just another beginning.

Morden as London's Not-Yet
in the spirit of experience
where the road forks as it narrows
into birdsongs of Landan creole
further straights into the path
walking home bound casting off rocks
I used to throw at myself i' th' Night.

The day break with freedom of choice
above self where the centre holds
into the periphery by design for living
this life in apposition. Morden, not yet.

If you defend the statue and offer it a milky bar
we ain't doing so well, we won't get on
so don't ask me to rise above the puddle of piss
this poem is a gun its onomatopoeia go ba ra ka.

I tested the rocket launcher
and the poem gathers momentum
before you know it (not just yet)
dickhead yaxley lennon's ear is all that remains
in your offering at the kabah for Nazis.

Beneath all this constant rage
is a deep wounding now I'm on crud
getting absolutely silly with it
wiggling because the poem has to rest
you try ketamize it but the nose knows
its blocked something about this inter
action with us is wrong
if we had common cause it would be better
but unfortunately you know about the Tudors
and the poem knows Toussaint, personally.

Th'overture reaches your enclosure
your pot calls the kettle white
mine makes a cup of splosh
and I sit by the river wandle
waiting for your amends.

If you want to know the ancestors
you don't need to keel over and die
just get to Morden and link a mate
talk to the anti-racist Irish Millwall fans
in Ganleys on a Tuesday or Thursday.
Morden is the place where people surprise
you constantly and you can remain teachable.

The anti-depressant turned me asigmatic
I want to be ante depression
and in Morden it feels possible
as my hairy nipples rest on the balcony.

Police dem get run out of ends
all stigma against South London
is manifestation of racism
Morden the root
Brixton the leaf
and Clapham full of yuppies
who will get drapes'd inshAllah.

From Lewisham McDeez
to the drive thru inna North Cheam
these A roads are cross sections
for us to stand in and extract the premium.
Boasty, spicy, lively, rowdy, poetry.

Art tells us now is the time
for the rupture to break the bitumen
letting the dust stay kicked up i'th'air
Sad faces pressed with rage
i'th'glass ceiling look so determined
change is healing and healing is painful
and that pain is addictive and addiction
is just our revolution against commodities.

trans-urban

we sat in commuter life sipping budvar fresh from plzen
thinking german purity laws as pharmakon
thinking bier frische crisp semi-jovial
transported through malayali beaches

where mayors sip whisky clandestinely under the palms
between clutched hands of homosocial parity
holidaying from london while the traces of CR0
remain palpably bedecked on the lips of chance encounter

the ghosts of discipling suggestiveness,
fishing coasts zoning in   taking earth's ends
ed roberson told us that
where interstitial being meets place-making

make meaning under the banana tree and hawthorn bush
the diaspora experiment cuts no ground,
following models of car wash
on slip roads beaten hard   and unsought tea

hamlet was made haider a poet on edge
made poet by edge and darkening reason
internalise the dissipating
gerund-lite existence

you sat thinking great expanse as south
london's horniman vegetal lavishness
kept us in retort replete with
corny healing and anglo pastorals

we were the natives and the cowboys
the frontier the scars along old kent rd
eating vegan sausages by the lake's breeze
cut between the lines of two systems

burn croydon //riots 2011//

just do it flying down the
street, broken shards
scattered, coppers
on the run, choppers
buzzing, screens
to the ready, fires burning
red sky at night, beds in
flames tigers
jumping breaking news

aged men speak
of times gone, blood and
rivers - white was not
black
black was
not white
codes in codes lost
in the post, hoods
looking for easy pickings, generation
wired bbm kfc jjb
i-riot   who
am i, mirror mirror
look at me riotous
indifference lol
whatever

sociologists puzzled tv

diatribe
headless youth workers
psycho -
geographies, sat navs
re-routing
dead zones of 'post-
industrial pastoral' – like
hell
bowling alone ikea b&q tgi
zone 5 carparks full, dogging
reality
bikers on the
edge, lost in overpass
under the fly, road
to nowhere

so fucking croydon
so fucking bowie
suburban sound, secret
times, punk rooted
brutalist dialectics unraveling
ballard, speculative
histories future noise
2-step to dubstep
beanos lost
in the concrete
jungle, cctv on guard, strike
a pose
kate moss

on the corners, tiger tiger
roaring sales, brit school dreams
fairfield retromania
st georges walk empty, peep
show at
home of dead babies

babel towers, nla, orbiting lunar
house, disappearing queues
forgotten arrivals, monstrous
plans left to rot
nf bnp edl on the
tram, sounding off going
viral, domes burn
unveiled threats, disappearing
jobs for the boys
class war, terry and june england
writing on the
wall
poems burn   ok

open//heart

   //in memory of the grenfell dead

*...there must have been an explosion, an irruption
somewhere, from the beginning of time, as time, and thus yet
beyond time, neither time nor not time, indeed displacing time,
before beginning, cavernous and massive, fractual, infinitely so;
an earthquake or a volcano; a black hole in the whiteness of being,
in the being of "whiteness ... for the disaster now and yet to come.*
                              //nahum chandler

the silence walked as if time had stopped
         out of time, the charred
      tower,   tomb to the dead,   a black
obelisk haunting   the city
      cries reverberating against the shattered
   dreams
   we came to live, and live,
and lived, we love
    and die, and die, and died together, tick
             tick
                 tick

my metallic heart valve   missed
     a   beat,   burning
              tower, heart bleeding,
remains remaining,   impotent TV
     simulacra,
cacophony of media
              guilt
       lost in the smoke of
                  hypocrisy
grieving souls,   sounding
          grievance, enclosed in furnaces of

98

speculative finance, flesh off
the bone, suffocating abodes, I can't
   breathe,
      cinders remain, lives   alone,
together, as one - you and me
                and us.

let them burn! rich stealing
                    life
white lies,   capital murder,   death
      traps, rage
rising, heart beating
faster

   Sunni said 'dad's death broke your heart'.

dad's open//broken heart,
dead migrants, dead labour, there is no fire

   without abstraction

tick tick   tick   broken-hearted,
the tower of anti//babel, the open//heart of
   Notting Hill refusing accumulation
by dispossession, dub step to other   syncopations
   in/formation, de-formation ---

       the bass   infrastructure of
sociality - opacity of nothingness -
      the dialectics of nothing is
more or less than 1
      the bleeding heart of
Handsworth 81, 85   the

                righteous rioting, babylon
facing the music, rastas I-an-I, steel pulse,
        Handsworth revolution, school discos,
            body talk,
broadway school, white flight
        lozells, aston, perry
barr, places that forgot time. Dad falls on the street
            lying on the hospital table, dad did not
rise.
workers poisoned in the factories of postimperial fordist
        death.

the machinic recalibration
        of immigrant souls,   invisible traces
    fold outside, small
                gestures of love//unity
    seize the time – in out of time Marvin 'what's going on?
Maze featuring Frankie Beverley, 'we are one'

LKJ told us a long time ago – Inglan is a Bitch,
   the ontological condition
            of the island race, drowning
in a sea of hate, opulence, indifference.
            st george
    soiled in the fakery of
deluded grandeur   caught in the

 banality of a not-so-new world order/
        built on virtual data, and tea at Fortnum and
Mason

the syntax of carnival revelry in the now-time
            of

      joy, undulating movements in the line, the 2nd
            line – can we feel
        the heart's
arrhythmic   pulsations, frequencies,   resonating

      the phonic flesh as Bacchannal

the heart ripped out, love of the in//operative
     multitude,
improvised
      inventive social poetics
   the opacity of the undercommons
        under erasure

For every Grenfell, fires burn. ashes to
     ashes
            from Dacca to Gaza, burning
   hell
Darwish: alas it was paradise.

 we run and
      run, shout, bass rumblings, open//heart(s), green
   heart
  with love and life...
         spacing the spaces of

     nothing,
haunted by the verticality
              of subprime
                      pressure

    we fly fuck dream dance riot   revolt
           memories of

futures   lost in time. why do you hate? when love is
     all we came with, we
          the abject labour of   whiteness
                         can you hear the beats of
     silence

                burning souls
          haunted tower   hedging capital
  tick

                tick

Acknowledgements

This publication constitutes an iteration of an ongoing collaboration which started at the Race, Poetry and Poetics in the UK conference at the University of Cambridge in 2018 titled 'Performing Thought: A collective poetics of mourning, (Asian) dislocation and the futurities of antiracism.' The second performance was held in Manchester as part of the Poetry Emergency Festival in 2019 titled 'Performing Thought 2.0.' Many thanks to the organisers.

Earlier versions of these poems have been published in *MOTE*, and *erotoplasty*. Many thanks to the editors.

www.ingramcontent.com/pod-product-compliance
Lightning Source LLC
Chambersburg PA
CBHW070103120526
44588CB00034B/2150